Here, Kitty!

FIREFLY BOOKS

Nicola Jane Swinney

A FIREFLY BOOK

Published by Firefly Books Ltd., 2019

Text © Nicola Jane Swinney

Copyright © QEB Publishing, Inc. 2017

First printing

Library of Congress Control Number: 2019938803

Library and Archives Canada Cataloguing in Publication

Title: Here, Kitty! / Nicola Jane Swinney.

Names: Swinney, Nicola Jane, author.

Description: Includes index.

Identifiers: Canadiana 20190098546 | ISBN 9780228102144 (softcover)

Subjects: LCSH: Cats—Juvenile literature. | LCSH: Cat breeds—Juvenile literature.

Classification: LCC SF445.7 .S95 2019 | DDC j636.8—dc23

Published in Canada by
Firefly Books Ltd.
50 Staples Avenue, Unit 1
Richmond Hill, Ontario
L4B 0A7

Published in the United States by
Firefly Books (U.S.) Inc.
P.O. Box 1338, Ellicott Station
Buffalo, New York
14205

Printed in China

Photographic Acknowledgments

Front cover: Getty Images/ULTRA.F
Back cover: Shutterstock/stockphoto-graf

bg = background, t = top, b = bottom, r = right, l = left, m = middle.

Adobe Stock: Manu29 36-37bg; seregraff 64-65bg; lafar256 68bl; GLS 70-71bg; coulanges 89br. **Alamy:** Juniors Bildarchiv GmbH 9br; 12-13bg, 13tr, 15tr, 15mr, 19br, 39tr, 45br, 73br, 78bl, 70tr, 92bl; WILDLIFE GmbH 10bl, 78-79bg; MJ Photography 12bl; Hemis 13br, 42bl; Arco Images GmbH 14-15bg, 15br, 24-25bg, 93br; Universal Images Group North America 14bl; blickwinkel 17tr, 61br, 68-69bg; Idamini 28-29bg, 29tr, 29mr; SUSAN LEGGETT 29br; Eugene Sergeev 38-39bg; Bonnie Nance/Dembinsky Photo 40-41bg; Fresh Start Images 41tr; Richard Peters 42-43bg; Tierphotoagentur 44bl, 46-47bg, 49mr, 58-59bg, 58bl, 67br, 77tr, 77br, 81tr, 87mr, 87br; Julie Thompson 49br; imageBROKER 56-57bg, 66-67bg; Mark J. Barrett 60bl; petographer 61tr; mauritius image GmbH 72bl; Mindy Fawver 74-75bg; Zoonar GmbH 77mr; Petra Wegner 80-81bg, 93tr; MARKA 83br; Sergey Taran 86-87bg; Zuzana Dolezalova 86bl; Suzanne Carlsson 87br. **Animal-Photography. com:** Alan Robinson 82-83bg; ally Anne Thompson 82bl; Helmi Flick 88-89bg, 89tr; Tetsu Yamazaki 90-91bg; Sally Anne Thompson 92-93bg. **Canstock:** fedcophoto 41br; byrdyak 54t; elzeva 80bl; epantha 94bl, 95br. **Dreamstime:** Tina Tang 9mr; Michael Przekop 18-19 bg; Sheila Bottoms 23br; Guy Zidel 24br; Ilongplay 25tr; Aliaksei Smalenski 25br; Onetouchspark 26bl; Annaav 27br; Buzzzikin 31br; Clement Morin 33br; Pavleta Radulova 37br; Sergey Taran 39br, 65tr; Jagodka 44-45bg; Treasuregirl79 46bl; Guinevra 49br; Chinook203 61mr; Juice Team 64bl; Linda Johnsonbaugh 66bl; Cynoclub 75tr; Susansanger 91br. **Edith Peulicke:** 32-33bg, 33tr, 33mr. **Getty Images:** Josef Timar 8bl; DEA/D. Mark Henrie 10-11bg; Robotti 11br; Auscape 19br; Michael Beder 63br; KIO 67tr; Tails 72-73bg; Satyendra Kumar Tiwari 89mr. **KimballStock:** Klein-Hubert 8-9bg, 60-61bg, 62-63bg; Chanan Photography 22-23bg. **Shutterstock:** otsphoto 1, 63br; Elisa Putti 2-3bg, 76-77bg; MNStudio 4-5bg; Sarah Fields Photography 6-7bg; Kyselova Inna 9tr; DrObjktiff 11br; vivver 16-17bg; Ivonne Wierink 16bl; Jagodka 17br; Natalia Fadosova 20-21bg, 30-31bg, 31mr; Patchaya Safari 22bl; Seregraff 26-27bg; dezi 27br, 51; milaphotos 31tr; Kseniia Kolesnikova 34-35bg; Natalie_Barth 37br; Ludmila Pankova 43br, 45tr; Linn Currie 43mr, 63mr; k45025 Rita K 43br; Windi Hissa 47tr; naD photos 47br; Serhii Moiseiev 50bg; frank60 50tl, 50tr; tankist276 52-53bg; Vasilyev Alexandr 53t; SV_zt 54bg; VLADIMIR LVP 54bl, 54br; Philip Kopylov 55bg; absolutimages 55tr; Mila Dubas 55br; Diana Taliun 59mr; Artur Marfin 62-63bg (wall); Best Dog Photo 65br; papa1266 69br; Scorpp 69br; Rika-Sama 73tr; Borkin Vadim 74br; TTstudio 79br; Pavel Sepi 81mr; Massimo Cattaneo 81br; Sezai Sahmay 84-85bg; Tatiana Makotra 90bl; Dmitriy Kostylev 91mr; Alex Papp 91br; KhingNarubas 94-95bg; Adisa 95tr; Stanislav Popov 96. **Superstock:** NaturePL 19mr; Biosphoto 22br; 48-49bg, Juniors 49tr; 59br; Gerard Lacz Images 83tr.

CONTENTS

ᴬ CAT BY OUR SIDE

Cats have been by our side as constant companions for thousands of years. When they were first domesticated cats were seen as useful animals rather than pets, but over the centuries that began to change. Although today's cats can be independent and adventurous, often preferring a roam around the neighborhood to a cuddle, they always find their way through the cat flap and back into their home to keep their owner company.

WORSHIPPED AND RESPECTED

Some of the first pet cats were owned by the ancient Egyptians. Many Egyptians were farmers, for whom rats and mice were a big problem. Cats killed many of the rodents that raided the farmers' grain stores, so cats became highly regarded. To the Egyptians, the cat was sacred, a creature to be worshipped and respected. Cats have never forgotten this... no other living animal can show disdain quite like the cat.

UTTER DELIGHT

If you've ever had a cat you will know just how many expressions these enigmatic animals can make. They range from disdain to utter delight to see you—even if it is just because it thinks you might have food to give. A cat might sometimes even refuse to meet your eye, especially if it is sitting in your seat or has just broken something! This range of reactions is part of their charm and is why we love them. But never think that you own a cat. The truth of the matter is that the cat owns you.

Ancient
Breeds

We think of cats as domestic animals, but don't be fooled—they share about 95.6 percent of their genes with tigers! They have only been kept as pets for the last 12,000 years or so, but some of our cats today share many features with those pets from the past.

THE ABYSSINIAN

With large ears and wide, almond-shaped eyes, the graceful Abyssinian resembles a small mountain lion. It has a triangular, expressive face and a sleek golden coat marked—or "ticked"—with black, which shimmers as the cat moves. Abyssinians look very much like the sacred cats that were worshipped by the ancient Egyptians.

AN ANCIENT BREED

Although its name comes from the part of north Africa now known as Ethiopia, the breed's roots are something of a mystery. Similar cats have been discovered in North Africa, Asia, and the Middle East, as well India and Indonesia. But no matter where it came from, the elegant cat soon found favor.

WILD ORIGINS

The first Abyssinian cat in England was probably one called Zula, who was brought from Ethiopia in 1868 by its owner. The breed was first mentioned in print in 1871, in a magazine article about the Crystal Palace Cat Show. It reported that an unusually marked cat had won third place. The cat had been imported from Abyssinia, and the name stuck.

FACT FILE

COLOR: ruddy, chocolate, cinnamon, blue, lilac, fawn, silver

EYE COLOR: gold, copper, green, hazel

SIZE (MALE ADULT): 10 pounds (4.5 kilograms)

LIFESPAN: 15 years

CHARACTER: lively, playful, affectionate

A PEOPLE PLEASER

Despite its rather wild appearance, the Abyssinian is a friendly, playful creature, whose joyful and lively antics have earned it the nickname "Aby-silly-an!" The cats are generally known as "Abys" by their fans, of whom there are many, and they like to be with their owners as much as possible.

THE CHARTREUX

Legend says that the Chartreux was kept as a mouser by Carthusian monks in France. Like the monks, who had taken a vow of silence, the cat is also extremely quiet! Instead of meowing, it chirps. Its origins probably lie in Persia (now Iran), and knights returning from the Crusades brought it back to France.

POTATO ON LEGS

Rather unkindly, the Chartreux is sometimes known as a "potato on toothpicks." Its well-built, solid body, with broad shoulders and deep chest, is supported by quite short, finely boned legs. However, one of its most endearing traits is its cheerful smile. Its rounded head and slightly indented forehead taper to a narrow muzzle, which makes it look like it is smiling.

SMOKY BLUE

The Chartreux's gorgeous fur is called blue, rather than gray, and has a woolly texture, with a soft undercoat to keep it warm. The earliest mention of these cats in France is from 1558, when a poet named Joachin de Bellay mourned the loss of his beloved cat Belaud. The Chartreux is an intelligent creature and enjoys human company, providing constant companionship.

ALMOST LOST

Many Chartreux were killed when World War II raged across Europe. To preserve the gene base, breeders introduced other cats, including blue British Shorthairs and Persians. But the breeders were clever and managed to keep the overall look of the Chartreux.

FACT FILE

COLOR: blue

EYE COLOR: gold to copper

SIZE (MALE ADULT):
   16 pounds (7 kilograms)

LIFESPAN: 15 years

CHARACTER: intelligent,
   friendly, affectionate

THE EGYPTIAN MAU

Pictures of heavily spotted cats—the forebears of today's handsome Mau—often appear in papyri and frescoes from ancient Egypt. These exotic creatures were the cats of pharaohs and kings, worshipped for their beauty. Research has shown that they originally came from the Fertile Crescent, a region that runs from the Nile River in Egypt to modern Iraq, Israel, Lebanon, Jordan, and Syria.

MYSTERIOUS MARKINGS

Today's Egyptian Mau has many of the traits of those early cats, including a "mascara marking" around its wide eyes, which are almond-shaped and slanted. This gives its charming face a rather worried look. Their eyes are a clear, pale green and the legs, tail, chest, and neck have bars of color, with a pattern often described as a "broken necklace."

A NATURAL ATHLETE

The Egyptian Mau has a lean, muscular body with a long flap of skin running from the end of its ribcage to its hind leg. This gives the animal an amazing ability to jump and allows it to move with great bursts of speed. The cat's hind legs are slightly longer than its front legs, so it appears to be standing on tiptoe. You can imagine these elegant cats posing as their subjects worship them!

A RAY OF SUNSHINE

The word "mau" means "sun" or "cat" in the language of ancient Egypt, and these affectionate cats bring a little sunshine with them. They can be shy of strangers at first, but will select their "special person" to dote on. Then they become very much part of the family, riding on shoulders, acting as a furry alarm clock, and generally being entirely interactive.

FACT FILE

COLOR: silver, bronze, smoke

EYE COLOR: green

SIZE (MALE ADULT):
  12 pounds (5.5 kilograms)

LIFESPAN: 15 years

CHARACTER: social, lively,
  doting

THE JAPANESE BOBTAIL

It is thought that the first domestic cats arrived on the islands of Japan with Buddhist monks around 600 A.D. to 700 A.D. They were used to keep rats and mice away from the rice paper scrolls kept in temples. A thousand years later, they were pressed into service in the thriving silk trade, protecting the delicate silkworms.

GOOD LUCK CHARM

Inquisitive and charming, the Japanese Bobtail soon came to represent good luck. Tri-colored—or calico—cats, known as *mi-ke* (pronounced "mee-kay"), were seen as especially lucky. A painting in the Smithsonian Institute from the 15th century shows two Japanese Bobtails, with their long coats parted down their backs and delightful pom-pom tails.

COMING TO AMERICA

Bobtails were imported to the United States in 1968 and became a recognized breed in 1979. Their engaging personality soon won them many fans, and their jaunty pompom tails—like a chrysanthemum in the longhaired cats—made them stand out.

HEALTHY AND STRONG

The Japanese Bobtail is a strong and muscular cat. Its hind legs are slightly longer than the front ones and the "Z" shape of the limbs gives the animal immense jumping power. They are less likely to suffer illnesses common in other cat breeds, and the kittens are large for newborns. They are active much earlier than many breeds, walk sooner, and get into trouble more quickly!

FACT FILE

COLOR: all colors, including mi-ke, rich red and black on a white background

EYE COLOR: all colors, including odd-eyed

SIZE (MALE ADULT): 10 pounds (4.5 kilograms)

LIFESPAN: 15 years

CHARACTER: friendly, playful, intelligent

THE SIAMESE

It looks like this beautiful cat is dressed for a fancy ball, in pale evening wear with chic dark accessories. But the Siamese isn't just beautiful—it is said to combine the grace of the panther, the speed of the deer, the strength of the tiger, the affection of the dog, and the courage of the lion.

THAI ORIGINS

The exact origins of the Siamese aren't clear, although it is known that similar cats existed in Siam (now Thailand) for centuries. These cats were pale-colored with dark "points"—ears, paws, tail, and "mask"—and brilliant blue eyes. The earliest mention is in *Cat Book Poems*, dating from 1350.

IMPORTANT POINTS

The striking cat arrived in the United States in 1879, when the U.S. Consul in Bangkok gave one to the wife of President Rutherford Hayes. At first, all cats classified as Siamese had a beige body with dark blackish-brown points. In later years, blue, chocolate, lilac, silver tabby, and smoke points were also accepted by the International Cat Association. It now accepts all colors and patterns.

ELEGANT ANGLES

Lively and talkative, the Siamese cat loves humans and needs people to thrive. Its glowing blue eyes are full of intelligence and emotion. Its head is gracefully triangular, with beautiful almond-shaped eyes and large upright ears. Its body is long and muscular, with long legs and a long tail. The Siamese is a creature of elegant angles.

FACT FILE

COLOR: seal point, chocolate point, blue point, lilac point, tabby point, red point, cream point, silver tabby point, smoke point, mixed-color point

EYE COLOR: blue

SIZE (MALE ADULT): 15 pounds (7 kilograms)

LIFESPAN: 15 years

CHARACTER: vocal, loving, playful

THE TURKISH ANGORA

Turkey's capital city, Ankara, used to be known as Angora, which is where this ancient breed gets its name. The cats' long, silky coats provided protection during harsh winters. The breed is thought to be related to the manul, a small wildcat that roamed Central Asia and Eurasia.

TREASURED BREED

Many owners of Angoras are proud of their cats, and some even consider themselves honored to own such a beautiful creature. However, the breed was once almost lost. The earliest written references to the cat are from 16th-century France, where it was crossed with other cats to breed Persian cats. As a breed on its own, it almost disappeared.

FACT FILE

COLOR: white, other solid colors

EYE COLOR: gold, green, blue, odd-eyed

SIZE (MALE ADULT):
9 pounds (4 kilograms)

LIFESPAN: 18 years

CHARACTER: intelligent, friendly, playful

BREEDING PROGRAM

In Turkey, a breeding program was set up at Ankara Zoo. The breeders concentrated on white cats with blue, gold, and odd eyes. In 1962, Ankara Zoo allowed Walter and Liesa Grant to take a male and female back to the United States. Named Yildiz and Yildizcek, these cats were the start of a new breed.

PLAYING HOST

The elegant Angora is known as the ballerina of the cat world, as it moves with athleticism and grace. It is energetic, which often gets it into trouble, and always ready to play. It loves people and wants attention, and will be determined to play "host" if you hold a party!

Rare
Breeds

Many cat breeds have evolved naturally, while others have been "helped" by human intervention. Some breeds today exist in very small numbers and it would be very sad if we were to lose this rich diversity.

THE BOMBAY

The stunning Bombay gets its name because it looks like a miniature version of the black leopards of India. These cats are always the densest, darkest midnight black with striking copper eyes, which are said to look like brand-new copper pennies. As well as its beauty, it has a charming nature, and is lively and affectionate.

BEAUTIFUL AND CALM

A fairly new breed, the Bombay was developed in 1953 by an American breeder named Nikki Horner. She wanted to produce a cat with sleek, shining fur and golden eyes that looked like a black leopard but had a calm temperament. She combined black American Shorthairs with Burmese cats and after many years finally achieved her goal.

NEW LINES

The Bombay was accepted by the cat organizations in the late 1970s and breeding programs continued. Later, American breeders Herb and Suzanne Zwecker developed new bloodlines with two cats called Shawnee and Road To Fame, which are found in Bombay pedigrees today.

A DELIGHTFUL PACKAGE

It has been said that if you want a dog, a cat, and a monkey all rolled into one mischievous package, the Bombay is the breed for you. These good-natured cats will enjoy your company, often sitting on your shoulder as you do your chores. They will greet you at the door and snuggle on your lap while you watch television. You'll never be lonely with a Bombay cat!

FACT FILE

COLOR: black

EYE COLOR: gold to copper

SIZE (MALE ADULT):
11 pounds (5 kilograms)

LIFESPAN: 16 years

CHARACTER: calm,
affectionate, loyal

THE CORNISH REX

The extraordinary-looking Cornish Rex is a new breed, like the Bombay, but it is the result of a natural change. In Cornwall, England, in 1950, a tortoiseshell cat called Serena gave birth to five kittens, one of which had an unusual velvet-soft curly coat. This little red-and-white kitten, named Kallibunker, would form the basis of the Cornish Rex.

CURLY COATS

Kallibunker's owner, Nina Ennismore, bred him back to his mother to continue the line. The mating produced three kittens, including two males with curly coats. Unfortunately, one of them died at seven months old, but the other curly kitten went on to father more litters. There were still very few like them, though, and the Cornish Rex became endangered.

STRONGER GENE POOL

Crosses with Siamese, Russian Blues, American and British Shorthairs, and Havanas were used to strengthen the breed's gene pool. In 1956 *Life* magazine ran a story about the curly-coated cats. A Californian named Frances Blancheri imported a pregnant female called LaMorna Cove, and began the Cornish Rex breed in the United States.

FACT FILE

COLOR: solid, silver, shaded

EYE COLOR: blue, green, gold

SIZE (MALE ADULT):
10 pounds (4.5 kilograms)

LIFESPAN: 15 years

CHARACTER: affectionate, clownish, energetic

ALWAYS A KITTEN

The Cornish Rex is certainly distinctive! A short, curly coat covers its Whippet-like slender body, and its large ears and round eyes make it look eternally inquisitive. It likes to be involved in everything you're doing and it never really loses its kittenish appeal—playing fetch, or using its agile paws to throw and catch objects.

THE DEVON REX

In the 1950s, a semi-wild tomcat living in an abandoned tin mine in the southwest of England fathered a litter of kittens with a tortoiseshell and white cat. One of the kittens had a dark brown curly coat just like his father's. Beryl Cox, who had adopted the female as a stray, kept the male kitten and named him Kirlee.

SAME, BUT DIFFERENT!

The county of Cornwall, on the southwest tip of England, is next to Devon, and Cox was aware of the work being done to produce the Cornish Rex. She contacted breeder Brian Sterling-Webb about Kirlee. Amazingly, he found that the gene that made Kirlee's coat so curly was different from the gene in his Cornish cousins.

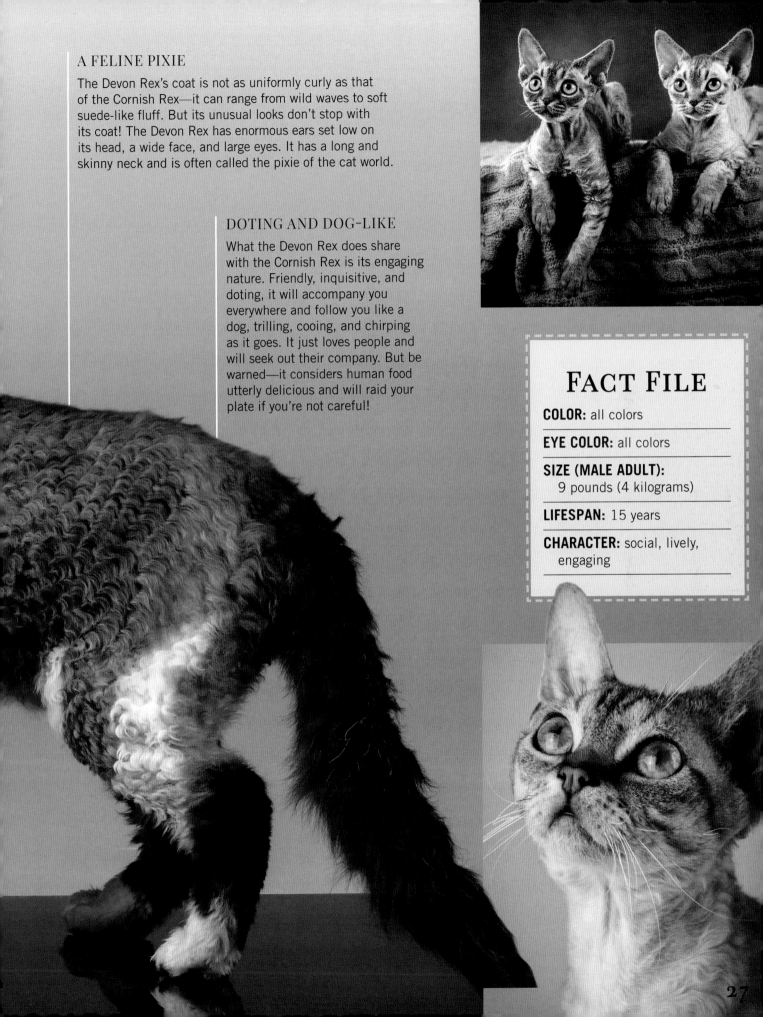

A FELINE PIXIE

The Devon Rex's coat is not as uniformly curly as that of the Cornish Rex—it can range from wild waves to soft suede-like fluff. But its unusual looks don't stop with its coat! The Devon Rex has enormous ears set low on its head, a wide face, and large eyes. It has a long and skinny neck and is often called the pixie of the cat world.

DOTING AND DOG-LIKE

What the Devon Rex does share with the Cornish Rex is its engaging nature. Friendly, inquisitive, and doting, it will accompany you everywhere and follow you like a dog, trilling, cooing, and chirping as it goes. It just loves people and will seek out their company. But be warned—it considers human food utterly delicious and will raid your plate if you're not careful!

FACT FILE

COLOR: all colors

EYE COLOR: all colors

SIZE (MALE ADULT):
9 pounds (4 kilograms)

LIFESPAN: 15 years

CHARACTER: social, lively, engaging

THE HIGHLANDER

Its solid, muscular body may resemble the wild lynx, but the Highlander—or Highland Lynx—has no wild cat in its makeup. It is a new breed with several traits that make it stand out. It has curling, tufted ears and a short, bobbed tail. Its feet often have more than the usual number of toes—a feature known as polydactyly.

BIG AND BRAWNY

The breed was started just after the new millennium, and the name "Highlander" was adopted in 2005. The cats are heavy-boned and brawny, with solid, muscular bodies under a thick coat of soft, dense fur. The breed is a mix of American Curl, English Manx, Abyssinian, and Bengal.

FACT FILE

COLOR: all colors

EYE COLOR: gold, green, blue

SIZE (MALE ADULT):
22 pounds (10 kilograms)

LIFESPAN: 16 years

CHARACTER: gentle, social, playful

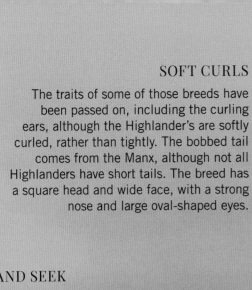

SOFT CURLS

The traits of some of those breeds have been passed on, including the curling ears, although the Highlander's are softly curled, rather than tightly. The bobbed tail comes from the Manx, although not all Highlanders have short tails. The breed has a square head and wide face, with a strong nose and large oval-shaped eyes.

HIDE AND SEEK

The Highlander loves to play, whether it's a game of tag or hide and seek. It is good with children and other pets, and can be taught to walk on a leash. Its boundless energy can get it into trouble. It is not very vocal, but it may chirp and coo when it wants your attention. You'll know if it's happy because it wags its short tail like a dog!

29

THE KURILIAN BOBTAIL

A chain of 56 volcanic islands between Russia and Japan is home to this curious creature. Cats with short tails are known to have existed on these islands for at least 200 years, and they were brought to Russia in the 20th century. There are fewer than 100 in North America, making them extremely rare.

UNIQUE TAIL

No two Kurilian Bobtail cats have exactly the same tail—it is as unique as a fingerprint. It looks like a pom-pom but there are lots of variations, including whisks, spirals, or brooms, and may consist of anywhere between two and ten vertebrae, kinked in different directions.

FACT FILE

COLOR: all colors

EYE COLOR: all colors, including odd-eyed

SIZE (MALE ADULT): 15 pounds (7 kilograms)

LIFESPAN: about 15 years

CHARACTER: gentle, intelligent, playful

STURDY AND STRONG

The Kurilian Bobtail is a large, solidly built cat with a rather wild appearance. It has a wide, rounded head, with big eyes and triangular ears. Its body is chunky and strong, with a broad chest and set on medium-length legs. The Bobtail is a very good jumper and likes to sit high up to watch over its domain.

A DEVOTED COMPANION

Intelligent, inquisitive, trainable, and gentle, the Kurilian breed just loves people. It will be devoted to its humans and happily follow them around, as well as sitting on laps and sleeping in beds if allowed! But it also has a natural instinct for hunting, like most cats.

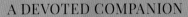

THE SOKOKE

The rarest breed of cat in the world takes its name from the Arabuko-Sokoko Forest Preserve, on the coast of Kenya in Africa. The local people call the cats "kadzonzo," which means "looks like tree bark." This is because the animal's ticked—or flecked—coat has a distinctive ring pattern.

CONQUERING DENMARK

Immediately recognizing that this was something unusual, Slater took a male and female kitten and hand-reared them. She then showed them to an acquaintance, Gloria Moeldrup, who later took a pair with her back to Denmark. They were shown in Copenhagen in 1984. By the year 2000, there were several breeding pairs in the country.

STRANGE KITTENS

In 1978, a Kenyan farmer named Jeni Slater was alerted to a litter of "strange kittens" by her gardener. "I went to investigate, and saw these huge eyes and big ears, and beautiful body markings," she recalled. This natural coat pattern is now being preserved through a deliberate breeding program, as these pretty cats are almost extinct in the wild.

FACT FILE

COLOR: tabby with ticking

EYE COLOR: amber to light green

SIZE (MALE ADULT): 11 pounds (5 kilograms)

LIFESPAN: 15 years

CHARACTER: independent, intelligent, energetic

LITTLE CHEETAH

Despite its wild roots, the Sokoke likes the company of people and will bond with its owner. It tends not to be a lap cat but will be interested in everything you do. And although it looks like a little cheetah, there is no aggression in the breed and it will get along happily with other household pets. It is slow growing, not reaching full maturity until the age of four or five.

American
Breeds

America is a land of innovators, so it's no surprise that many cat
breeds began in the United States. Many of these new varieties were
bred to be affectionate and gentle, and they have been recognized
by the various cat breed associations.

THE AMERICAN BOBTAIL

This attractive creature has the look of the bobtailed wildcat about it, but it is a natural cat breed that is gentle and loving and will bond with its owner. The first recorded American Bobtail was a stray called Yodi that was adopted by John and Brenda Sanders, who found him on a Native American reservation.

UNUSUALLY SHORT TAIL

When Yodi mated with John and Brenda's non-pedigree cat, Mishi, the resulting kittens had their father's unusually short tail. The Sanders' friends, Mindy Schultz and Charlotte Bentley, took several of the kittens and bred the first true American Bobtails. The breed was recognized by the International Cat Association in 1989.

TRAVELING CATS

Those early bobtailed cats were crossbred with other cats who combined a sturdy build and short tail with a sweet and loving nature. The American Bobtail is a particularly good-natured animal. Long-distance truckers have found the cat to be an excellent traveling companion, perfectly happy to sit with them in the cab.

FACT FILE

COLOR: black, blue, brown, chocolate, cream, fawn, white

EYE COLOR: all colors

SIZE (MALE ADULT):
16 pounds (7 kilograms)

LIFESPAN: 15 years

CHARACTER: intelligent, gentle, loving

A SOLID RECTANGLE

A Bobtail's famous short tail may be straight, curved, kinked, or have bumps along its length. It is flexible and expressive—you can tell if your Bobtail is happy by looking at its tail! But the breed has other traits, too. It is a generally solid, rectangular cat, with a broad chest, prominent shoulder blades, muscular legs, and a wide wedge-shaped head.

THE AMERICAN CURL

All American Curl cats can be traced back to a stray black kitten called Shulamith, found by Californian couple Joe and Grace Ruga. They discovered the longhaired kitten on their doorstep in 1981 and fell in love with her silky coat and unusually curled ears. When Shulamith had her first litter of kittens six months later, two of them had those distinctive ears.

ADORABLE EARS

The kittens' father was unknown but the Rugas asked for advice from an expert, who looked into the gene that caused the backward-curling ears. This gene was dominant—meaning that only one parent needed to have it to pass on the trait. Starting in 1983, American Curl cats were bred selectively, to ensure the new breed always had those adorable ears.

SILKY COAT

American Curl kittens are born with straight ears, but they start to curl in just a few days. The cats also have an expressive face with large round eyes, and a silky coat that comes in both longhaired and shorthaired versions. It has very little undercoat, so it doesn't need much grooming and doesn't shed too much.

FACT FILE

COLOR: all colors

EYE COLOR: all colors

SIZE (MALE ADULT):
10 pounds (4.5 kilograms)

LIFESPAN: 16 years

CHARACTER: intelligent, loving, good with children

FAMILY PET

The American Curl is the perfect pet for a family—it adores human company and, unusually for a cat, loves children. It is very people-oriented and will happily follow you around all day, occasionally demanding attention but mostly just "helping" you. American Curls never completely lose their kittenish behavior and because of that are known as the "Peter Pan of the cat world."

THE AMERICAN SHORTHAIR

The first "native" breed of cat in the United States may have arrived in Massachusetts with the Pilgrims aboard the *Mayflower*, which sailed from Plymouth, England, in 1620. No cats were listed on the ship's manifest, but it was common to have cats on board to kill rodents.

EXCELLENT RATTERS

Whether or not there were actually cats on the *Mayflower*, what is certain is that the ratting abilities of those first cats were later recognized by farmers and store owners, and the cats became essential members of the community. Those that had survived the long sea journey were, by necessity, fit and hardy.

VALUABLE CATS

Their hunting talent was praised in a publication in 1634, in which the cats were credited with saving a New England settlement's crops from greedy squirrels and chipmunks. In 1895, the American Shorthair was exhibited at the first ever cat show in the United States. The following year, an American Shorthair was offered for sale at $2,500—a dizzyingly enormous amount of money at the time.

SWEET NATURE

Originally called the domestic shorthair, the breed was one of the first five to be registered by the Cat Fanciers' Association in 1906. The name changed to American Shorthair in 1966. It is a handsome, medium-sized cat whose wide, open face has a sweet expression, and the cat has a sweet nature to match. It has never lost its ability to hunt but will happily play with toys.

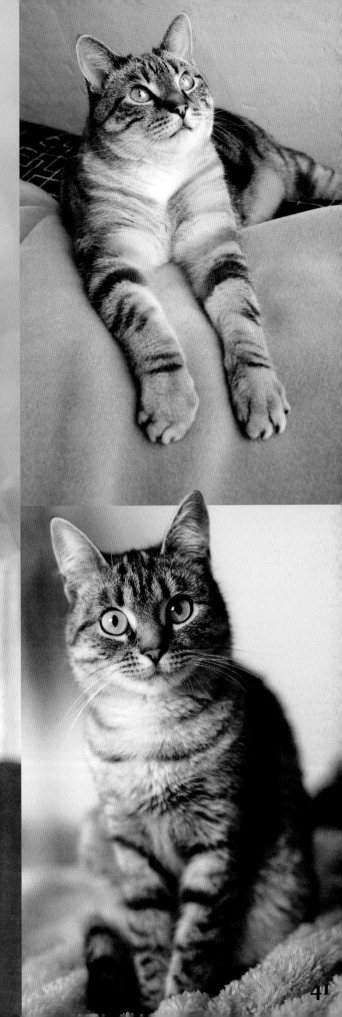

FACT FILE

COLOR: all colors

EYE COLOR: all colors

SIZE (MALE ADULT):
14 pounds (6 kilograms)

LIFESPAN: 20 years

CHARACTER: playful, happy, sweet-tempered

THE RAGDOLL

This charming breed—developed in the 1960s—got its name because it will happily flop into your arms or at your feet, limp like a doll. Some owners have even dressed their cats in doll's clothes and carried them around! The Ragdoll's laid-back attitude has made this adorable breed a favorite all over the world.

THE FIRST RAGDOLL

The breed was developed by Ann Baker of California, using a pure white longhaired female. She bred one of the cat's daughters, Buckwheat, to a male. The male was mitted, meaning that it had white feet, as if wearing socks. Baker also used Buckwheat's half-sister Fugianna to form the foundation of the breed that she called "Ragdoll."

FACT FILE

COLOR: four recognized patterns, but most colors

EYE COLOR: blue

SIZE (MALE ADULT): 20 pounds (9 kilograms)

LIFESPAN: 17 years

CHARACTER: laid-back, affectionate, cuddly

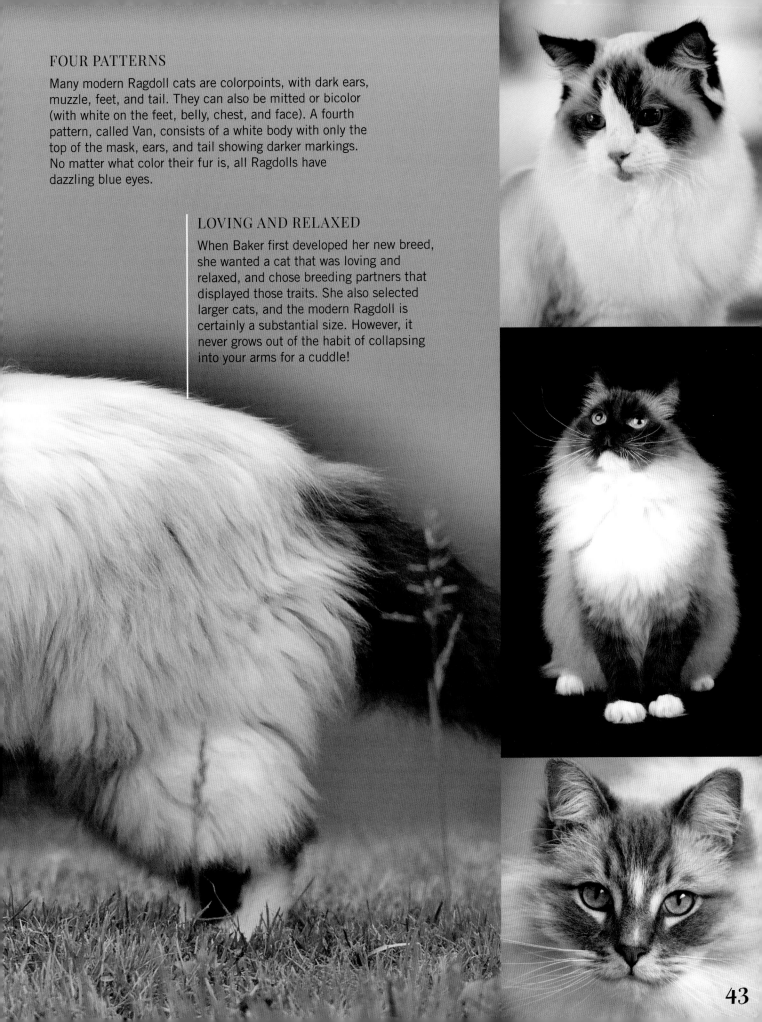

FOUR PATTERNS

Many modern Ragdoll cats are colorpoints, with dark ears, muzzle, feet, and tail. They can also be mitted or bicolor (with white on the feet, belly, chest, and face). A fourth pattern, called Van, consists of a white body with only the top of the mask, ears, and tail showing darker markings. No matter what color their fur is, all Ragdolls have dazzling blue eyes.

LOVING AND RELAXED

When Baker first developed her new breed, she wanted a cat that was loving and relaxed, and chose breeding partners that displayed those traits. She also selected larger cats, and the modern Ragdoll is certainly a substantial size. However, it never grows out of the habit of collapsing into your arms for a cuddle!

43

THE SELKIRK REX

With its thick, woolly coat, the Selkirk Rex is sometimes called a "cat in sheep's clothing." The curly fur is the result of a natural genetic mutation, the same as in the Cornish and Devon Rex. But unlike those breeds, the gene that causes the curl in the Selkirk Rex is dominant, meaning that curly-coated and straight-coated kittens can be born in the same litter.

WANTING ATTENTION

In 1987, a cat breeder named Jeri Newman came across a strange-looking kitten in a litter born to a stray cat. She named the kitten Miss DePesto because she was always pestering her for attention. The kitten had curly whiskers, wiry hair in her ears, and a wavy coat. Newman was a breeder of Persian cats and when the kitten was old enough, she bred her to a black Persian.

WHY SELKIRK?

Miss DePesto had six kittens, three of which had curly coats—and the Selkirk Rex breed was born. Newman chose "Selkirk" because it was the name of her stepfather, making it the only current breed to be named after a person. Persians and British and Exotic Shorthairs were used to continue the breed, and both short and longhaired varieties occur naturally.

FACT FILE

COLOR: all colors

EYE COLOR: all colors

SIZE (MALE ADULT):
15 pounds (7 kilograms)

LIFESPAN: 15 years

CHARACTER: gentle, placid, loving

CURLY WHISKERS

Newman wanted the Selkirk Rex to be a robust, well-built, yet placid cat. It takes time to mature and is not as vocal as some breeds, but it is sweet-tempered and cuddly. The shorthair version is like a stuffed animal, while the longhaired Selkirk has loose waves of silky fur. The kittens can be easily identified at birth because they are born with curly whiskers.

THE SNOWSHOE

A few early photographs show Siamese kittens with four white feet, and a white-pawed Siamese was reported in the 1950s. However, it was not until the 1960s that the Snowshoe breed was developed, when a breeder named Dorothy Hinds-Daugherty decided to create a cat that had the elegant Siamese colored points as well as white paws.

BEST OF BOTH

Hinds-Daugherty had bred a litter of Siamese kittens, three of which had four white paws. When they were old enough, she bred them to an American Shorthair that had tuxedo markings—black coat with a white belly, chest, throat, and paws. The result was an attractive cat with striking markings and the best features of both breeds. She named it Snowshoe.

FACT FILE

COLOR: all pointed colors, several patterns

EYE COLOR: blue

SIZE (MALE ADULT):
12 pounds (5.5 kilograms)

LIFESPAN: 19 years

CHARACTER: loving, playful, smart

NEVER MEAN

Each Snowshoe cat is as unique as a snowflake, with its own personality and coloring. But they all have a lighter colored body, dark points, white feet, and a distinct upside-down "V" between their eyes. Their personality can be confident or shy, quiet or talkative, bossy or placid, but these pretty little cats are never mean. And they will act like they own you—not the other way around!

ALMOST LOST

Despite the success of those early breeding attempts, poor record-keeping and waning interest meant the Snowshoe was almost lost. By 1977, there was only one person in the United States breeding Snowshoe cats. Luckily, the breed regained its popularity, and by 1989 there were 30 breeders.

THE MAINE COON

Many Maine Coon owners swear that they would never want a different breed! The Maine Coon is the largest breed of pet cat, with a chunky build, broad back, and sturdy legs. Its large body is covered in a gorgeous shaggy coat made up of a mix of different lengths of hair.

A QUEEN'S CAT

One legend says that the queen of France, Marie Antoinette, sent her cats to America, where they mixed with local breeds to produce the first Maine Coons. The reason they are called "Coons" is a bit of a mystery. The look of the early Maine Coons—brown tabbies with black facial markings and a ringed tail—led to the myth that the breed was the result of cats mating with raccoons. However, this is not true.

BEST CAT

A handsome black-and-white cat called Captain Jenks of the Horse Marines is the subject of the first written reference to a Maine Coon cat in 1861. In 1895 a female Maine Coon called Cosie was named best cat at a show held in Madison Square Garden, New York. In the best tradition, she was a brown tabby.

FACT FILE

COLOR: all colors

EYE COLOR: blue, green, gold

SIZE (MALE ADULT):
22 pounds (10 kilograms)

LIFESPAN: 16 years

CHARACTER: affectionate, clever, vocal

GENTLE GIANT

Today's Maine Coons come in all sorts of colors, including blue-eyed grays and orange-eyed creams. Adult males can reach 25 pounds (11 kilograms) in weight, but this is a gentle giant that loves to play and will follow you around like a dog. It can even be taught to play fetch and to walk on a leash!

Cuddly Kittens

What could be more adorable than a litter of little kittens? You could spend hours watching kittens at their rough-and-tumble play—but it's not just for fun. The kitten is learning how to be a cat. Every pounce is teaching it how to hunt; every high-pitched squeak an experiment in communication. During those first few months, the kitten is preparing to face the big wide world.

SETTLING SOMEWHERE SAFE

Female cats are known as queens, while males are toms. Queens can become pregnant from the age of just four months and the breeding season runs from February until August. In cats, pregnancy lasts for 63 to 65 days—a time known as the gestation period. During the last few weeks, the queen will start looking for somewhere safe to have her babies.

LITTERS

The number of kittens per litter can range from one to nine, though four or five are more usual. The most kittens in one litter ever recorded was 19, born to a Siamese-Burmese cat in England in 1970. Cats are generally very good mothers and as soon as the babies are born, the queen will check them over and lick them clean.

MOTHER'S FIRST MILK

Kittens will start to feed from their mother quickly after birth because they need lots of nourishment right away. The first milk she gives them is vital—it is called "colostrum" and is rich with antibodies that fight diseases. It will help the babies to grow strong and healthy.

53

GAINING WEIGHT

New kittens will need to feed every two or three hours, and for the first three or four weeks of their lives they spend much of the rest of the time asleep. When they are born, they weigh between 3 and 4 ounces (90 to 110 grams). But they grow quickly, gaining up to half an ounce (15 grams) in weight every day. They should be double their birth weight by the time they are two weeks old.

PLAYING AND LEARNING

As they grow in size and bravery, the queen teaches her kittens how to be cats. She will help them understand how to use their litter tray, and they will start to learn hunting skills. Kittens are naturally inquisitive and will happily play all day—or until they get tired and fall asleep, often in the most unlikely places! But their games will teach them how to interact and how to communicate.

READY TO ROAM

The kittens should be weaned from their mother—no longer relying on her for food—by the time they are seven or eight weeks old, although some stay with their mother for longer. They are then ready to go to a loving home, where a life of adventure and affection awaits!

Unusual
Breeds

A pet cat is a familiar sight, but some breeds can look rather odd! Many have developed naturally, adopting their strange look for practical reasons. Others have been bred deliberately for those unusual but endearing traits.

THE RUSSIAN BLUE

This gorgeous cat, with its shimmering silver-blue coat and sparkling green eyes, is sometimes called the Archangel cat, because it came from the Russian port of Arkhangelsk on the White Sea. It adapted to the long, harsh winters of northern Russia by growing a plush, thick coat.

TIPPED WITH SILVER

The short, bright blue coat is tipped with silver that reflects the light and shimmers like silk as the cat moves. Its coat stands out from its body, and if you draw patterns in the fur with your finger, they will stay there until you smooth them out again. Although the coat is short, it is dense and soft, and sheds very little.

LIKE A WILD RABBIT

The silver-blue cats soon found their way to England and northern Europe—probably on ships sailing from Arkhangelsk. One was exhibited at the Crystal Palace Cat Show in 1875 as the Archangel, competing against other blue-coated breeds. A newspaper reported that the Russian Blue was "very furry" and "resembled mostly the wild gray rabbit."

FACT FILE

COLOR: blue

EYE COLOR: green

SIZE (MALE ADULT):
13 pounds (6 kilograms)

LIFESPAN: 15 years

CHARACTER: intelligent, playful, sensitive

STRIKINGLY HANDSOME

The new breed was soon established in England and was imported to the United States. After World War II it was revived by using Siamese and British Blue bloodlines. The modern Russian Blue is a strikingly handsome cat, with an intelligent and charming nature that makes it a popular companion as well as a hard-to-beat show cat.

THE MANX

According to one legend, Noah shut the door on the tail of the Manx cat as it boarded the ark before the great flood. But the truth is that the animal's missing tail is likely a natural development. And since the breed comes from an island (the Isle of Man, near England) there was no crossbreeding with other cats, so the breed kept its tailless appearance.

NORWEGIAN CATS

The first picture of a tailless cat on the Isle of Man was painted in 1810, but these cats existed at least as far back as 1750. They were originally shorthaired, but there are now longhaired Manx cats too—possibly as a result of mixing with Norwegian Forest Cats brought to the island by Viking settlers. Longhaired Manx cats are known as Cymrics, but the two kinds are the same breed.

LIKE A BOWLING BALL

The Manx is a medium-sized cat, often compared to a bowling ball because of its wide, round face. Most have a missing tail, although some have short, stumpy tails and some are born with full-length tails. The Manx's hind legs are longer than its front ones, so its rump is higher than its head.

BUNNY CAT

The uneven legs give the Manx a hopping style of walking. This hopping movement, combined with the short or missing tail, gave rise to a theory that the Manx was the result of a cat mating with a rabbit, which is not true. But it earned the Manx the nickname "bunny cat." The name suggests a cuddly creature, which the Manx certainly is—gentle and loving, but ready to play.

FACT FILE

COLOR: all colors

EYE COLOR: all colors

SIZE (MALE ADULT):
12 pounds (5.5 kilograms)

LIFESPAN: 14 years

CHARACTER: gentle, affectionate, intelligent

61

THE MUNCHKIN

These cats are the feline equivalent of a Dachshund—adorably cute, endlessly appealing, but with very short legs. Short-legged cats naturally appear sometimes but the Munchkin cat is a relatively new breed. In the past few years breeders have been deliberately producing these tiny cats.

STUMPY LIMBS

A British veterinary report in 1944 noted four generations of short-legged cats, with the only difference between them and other cats being their stumpy limbs. No one knows what became of those cats, but the accepted foundation for the modern Munchkin was a black female called Blackberry. She gave birth to a litter of short-legged cats.

ACCEPTABLE BREED?

The Munchkin has been the subject of much debate. Even though its short legs are caused by a natural mutation of a gene, some say it is cruel to deliberately try to breed short-legged cats. The International Cat Association has accepted the Munchkin, although other groups have not. The cats do not appear to suffer any more than other breeds, or any more than short-legged dog breeds.

FACT FILE

COLOR: all colors

EYE COLOR: all colors

SIZE (MALE ADULT):
9 pounds (4 kilograms)

LIFESPAN: 13 years

CHARACTER: lively, playful, friendly

LITTLE MAGPIE

As for personality, the Munchkin doesn't seem to know how small it is! It is sometimes called the "magpie of the cat world" because it loves shiny objects and will often "borrow" them and hide them to play with later. And these little cats love to play—with other cats, children, and even friendly dogs.

THE SPHYNX

The first known Sphynx cat was called Prune, a fitting name for this alien-looking wrinkled creature! They are often described as hairless, but the body of the Sphynx is, in fact, covered with very fine, downy fuzz. This gives it a texture that is pleasantly soft to the touch.

WARM SKIN

The other thing you will notice when you touch a Sphynx is how warm it is—up to four degrees warmer than other felines. Yet the first Sphynx cats came from Canada, where a thick fur coat would have been more practical! The breed was once known as the Canadian hairless cat before it was changed to "Sphynx," after the massive Egyptian sculpture.

HAIRLESS KITTENS

Prune, the first Sphynx, was one of a litter born to a black-and-white cat called Elizabeth. Prune was later bred to other cats in an effort to reproduce more hairless kittens, with some success. The breed's founding fathers are generally accepted to be three hairless kittens called Epidermis, Punky, and Paloma.

FACT FILE

COLOR: all colors

EYE COLOR: all colors

SIZE (MALE ADULT):
12 pounds (5.5 kilograms)

LIFESPAN: 14 years

CHARACTER: loving, playful, intelligent

CHARMING FACE

It's not just its "baldness" that makes the Sphynx stand out. Its enormous ears frame a charming face, with large eyes and a sweet expression. It comes in a variety of colors, for which the pigment is in the skin as well as the fine covering of down. It tends to get cold but is clever enough to find a warm spot, perhaps in the sunshine or even on a computer!

THE SAVANNAH

The Savannah is a cross between an African wild cat called a serval and a domestic cat. It has the lean, muscular grace of a leopard, the beauty of a cheetah, and the gentle nature of a pet tabby. The founder of this striking breed was a kitten born in 1966. She was called Savannah and gave her name to these glorious cats.

AFRICAN GRASSLANDS

Breeders Patrick Kelly and Joyce Sroufe joined forces to develop the Savannah breed, whose name echoes the wild tree-scattered grasslands of Africa. They started with an offspring from that first kitten. Bengals and Egyptian Maus, as well as some shorthaired breeds, were used in those early days.

WILD AND EXQUISITE

The breeders' goal was to produce a wild-looking cat that resembled the serval but had a calm and even temper. Of all the cat breeds, the Savannah is arguably the most exquisite. Elegant and graceful, it has a long neck, slender legs, and huge ears. It features in the Guinness Book of World Records as the world's tallest domestic cat.

WATER LOVER

A Savannah's markings include spots that stand out against its paler coat, "tear stain" markings running from its large, expressive eyes, and a ringed tail. It is a highly intelligent and inquisitive cat that wants to play. Unlike most cats, it loves water, and will happily walk on a leash. If you want a quiet cat, choose a different breed, but who can resist the unique Savannah?

FACT FILE

COLOR: brown, silver, black, smoke

EYE COLOR: all colors

SIZE (MALE ADULT): 20 pounds (9 kilograms)

LIFESPAN: 20 years

CHARACTER: intelligent, curious, playful

THE SCOTTISH FOLD

A shepherd named William Ross found the first Scottish Fold on a farm in Coupar Angus, Scotland, in 1961. It was a white longhaired barn cat called Susie, and her unusual ears were folded forward and flat to the top of her head. When Susie had a litter of kittens, Ross adopted one. Today, all Scottish Folds can be traced back to Susie.

SWEET FACE

In developing the new breed, Ross used Persians, American Shorthairs, Exotic Shorthairs, and even Burmese to achieve the sweet expression of the Scottish Fold. Under its cap-like folded ears, it is a rounded creature, with a round face, round eyes, and a round body. There are shorthaired and longhaired versions, although the longhaired cats are known as Coupari in Canada.

FACT FILE

COLOR: all colors

EYE COLOR: all colors but copper is the most common

SIZE (MALE ADULT):
12 pounds (5.5 kilograms)

LIFESPAN: 14 years

CHARACTER: social, gentle, playful

A STRAIGHT START

All Scottish Fold kittens are born with straight ears that start to curl after about three weeks. The gene that causes this is recessive, meaning that both parents must carry it to have offspring with folded ears. The folds range from a loose single fold to a tight "triple" one.

FAMOUS FANS

Some people worry that the Scottish Fold is prone to ear problems, although breeders deny this. The breed is popular in the United States, where celebrities such as Taylor Swift are among its fans. As well as its unusual appearance, this appealing cat often adopts the "Buddha pose," where it sits like a human, with its hind legs stuck out in front.

Longhaired
Breeds

For some cat breeds, their natural beauty is enhanced by a long, flowing coat. Longhaired cats have been around for centuries and are prized the world over. They come in all shapes and sizes, colors, and characters.

THE BALINESE

How do you make a Siamese cat even more striking? The answer is simple—give it a long, silky coat. Longhaired Siamese have been around for centuries. One appears on an ancient Chinese tapestry, a magazine published in 1871 makes reference to one, and one was registered in 1928.

GRACEFUL DANCERS

The appearance of a longhaired Siamese was likely a genetic quirk, with litters of kittens containing one every so often. But in the 1950s, two breeders in the United States decided to produce the longhaired cats deliberately. They chose the name "Balinese" to reflect the graceful dancers of Bali.

FACT FILE

COLOR: seal, blue, chocolate, lilac, red, cream, tortoiseshell, tabby, bicolor

EYE COLOR: blue

SIZE (MALE ADULT):
10 pounds (4.5 kilograms)

LIFESPAN: 15 years

CHARACTER: intelligent, playful, attentive

SIAMESE COLORS

The long hair of the Balinese lies closely against its body and doesn't mat. It flows along the sleek lines of the cat, with the tail forming a luxurious plume. The first Balinese had coats in the four recognized color points of the Siamese—seal, blue, chocolate, and lilac. Cats with long coats in other colors were called Javanese, though the two breeds were merged in 2008.

LOVELY PERSONALITY

While it is one of the most beautiful cat breeds, the Balinese is also a lovely animal to have around. It is not as vocal as its Siamese cousin but is just as opinionated! It will follow you as you do your chores too, and expect to be on your lap when you stop for a coffee break. The Balinese loves to be loved!

THE BIRMAN

There is a Burmese legend about a golden-eyed white cat that stood guard over its dying master. Its head, legs, and tail turned dark brown as its master died, but its feet and ankles stayed pure white as its master's soul passed to the cat. Its eyes turned sapphire blue, the same as the goddess who waited to lead its master to the next world.

SACRED CAT

Because of this legend, the Birman is sometimes called the Sacred Cat of Burma. The story came from the priests of Burma, but little more is known. Most American Birmans can be traced to England, France, Australia, and Germany. Its personality is said to reflect those countries: English dignity, French flair, an Australian sense of adventure, and German patience.

FACT FILE

COLOR: all colorpoints

EYE COLOR: blue

SIZE (MALE ADULT):
12 pounds (5.5 kilograms)

LIFESPAN: 16 years

CHARACTER: gentle, sweet, friendly

FAMILY PET

Those traits made the Birman one of the world's favorite cat breeds. Not only is it a creature of considerable beauty, but it is also a friendly, sociable animal that makes a great family pet. It can be quite chatty, but not very loud. It enjoys human company and is good with small children, since it has a tolerant nature.

ROMAN NOSE

Seen in profile, the Birman's "Roman nose" comes out from the cat's forehead and rises in a smooth bump before tapering at the tip. The face is broad, with ears that are almost as wide as they are tall, giving the cat a sweet expression. Like all pointed breeds, Birman kittens are born white.

THE NORWEGIAN FOREST CAT

A big, strong body with a thick, fluffy coat meant the Norwegian Forest Cat could travel with the Vikings. These hardy explorers valued the breed for its ability to keep ships and villages free of rats and mice. The Vikings called these prized felines "skotgatt," which translates as "forest cat."

A LEGENDARY CAT

Norwegian Forest Cats appear in Viking mythology, including the legend that six giant cats pulled the chariot of Freya, the goddess of love. The sturdy Norwegian Forest Cat would probably be strong enough! Its exact origins are unclear—it may be related to the Siberian cat from Russia, where its thick coat would have provided protection from the harshest weather.

ROYAL APPROVAL

When World War II broke out, the Norwegian Forest Cat was almost lost. Attempts to save the breed proved successful, and it was later made the official cat of Norway by King Olaf V. The breed was not exported to the United States until the late 1970s, but it is now one of the most popular breeds.

HANDSOME AND CHARMING

Some people mistake the Norwegian Forest Cat for a Maine Coon, and the two do look similar. In fact, DNA testing has proved that the breeds are related. The Norwegian version has a more triangular face than the Maine Coon, with almond-shaped eyes. It is hard not to fall for the charms of this handsome cat!

FACT FILE

COLOR: all colors

EYE COLOR: all colors

SIZE (MALE ADULT):
18 pounds (8 kilograms)

LIFESPAN: 16 years

CHARACTER: smart, independent, sociable

THE PERSIAN

The Persian has long, luxuriant fur and a sweet face, adorned with wide eyes and an air of aloof nobility, making it the ultimate glamour-puss. The Persian is one of the oldest breeds in the world, appearing in ancient Egyptian hieroglyphs from as early as 1684 B.C.

PRECIOUS CARGO

One legend says that this beautiful cat was hidden in camel caravans containing jewels and precious spices that traveled from Persia (modern-day Iran). The cats were called Persian after the country they came from, and quickly became prized. They were brought to Europe in 1626 by an Italian nobleman named Pietro Della Valle.

CELEBRITY CATS

Cat shows became popular in the late 1800s, and the first big championship in England was held at Crystal Palace in 1871. Cats from Persia, Turkey, and Afghanistan were shown together as "Asian breeds." Queen Victoria was a fan of the exotic Persian and it soon became a must-have among English gentry.

GRACEFUL JEWEL

The first Persians were silver-gray, but the breed now comes in all colors, and has a much rounder face. It has a delightful snubbed nose, chubby cheeks, and small ears. It is a stocky creature, with rather short legs and a sturdy body. The Persian is quiet and dignified, and it adorns any room it chooses to grace with its presence.

FACT FILE

COLOR: all colors

EYE COLOR: copper, blue, green, odd-eyed

SIZE (MALE ADULT):
12 pounds (5.5 kilograms)

LIFESPAN: 14 years

CHARACTER: quiet, gentle, intelligent

THE SIBERIAN

The Siberian is a Russian national treasure. The earliest known reference to a longhaired Russian cat is from 1000 A.D., and they have existed in Russian fairy tales and folklore ever since. The modern breed is a large barrel-shaped cat with strong legs to support its large frame and huge paws that would be the envy of a heavyweight boxer!

FLUFFY PANTALOONS

Siberia is the most northern part of Russia, extending east from the Ural Mountains, all the way to the Pacific Ocean. Siberia's native cat breed has a rich, full triple coat to protect it from sub-zero temperatures, with a thick ruff around the neck, fluffy "pantaloons" on its hind legs, and a full bushy tail. It sometimes wraps its tail around its face and paws for extra warmth.

ATHLETIC CAT

The Siberian is a highly intelligent cat that will soon figure out how to open doors, find its way into the food container for a quick snack, and engage you in a game of fetch. In spite of its large size, it is very athletic and will climb trees or the highest point in a room. And it loves playing with—and in—water!

WARM HEART

It is said that the Siberian cat's heart is as warm as its homeland is cold. It is true that the Siberian is a cat that loves people and wants to be with them. It is not shy with strangers and it is happy to play host, chatting away in charming trills and chirps. It tends not to be as needy as some breeds, but will welcome your attention when you're ready for snuggles.

FACT FILE

COLOR: all colors

EYE COLOR: all colors, including odd eyes

SIZE (MALE ADULT): 17 pounds (7.5 kilograms)

LIFESPAN: 15 years

CHARACTER: calm, easygoing, playful

THE TURKISH VAN

Don't be surprised if you find your Turkish Van happily splashing in the garden pond or joining you in the bath—this is a cat that loves water! It takes its name from Lake Van in Turkey, from where it is thought to originate. Although it is equally ancient, it is completely different from Turkey's other native cat, the Angora.

FROM THE ARK

The Turkish Van's waterproof coat has a texture like the softest cashmere. Legend says that the Turkish Van swam ashore from Noah's ark, which ran aground on Mount Ararat in Turkey—not far from Lake Van. Another legend says that a door on the ark slammed on the cat's tail, turning it red, and God touched its head to give it a matching color.

STRIKING BREED

The isolation of the Turkish Van's mountainous home meant that the breed stayed pure. It wasn't until the 1950s that it was brought to the West. Two tourists discovered the unusually marked cats and took two kittens, a male and a female, home with them. They then promoted the striking breed in England.

NATIONAL TREASURE

The breed is admired for its shimmering white coat and richly colored head and tail—a combination known as the Van pattern. Its fur is extremely soft and its tail is magnificently plumed. The Turkish Van is a curious, active creature that loves running and climbing, as well as human company. No wonder it is considered a national treasure in its native Turkey!

FACT FILE

COLOR: white with colored patches

EYE COLOR: blue, amber, odd-eyed

SIZE (MALE ADULT): 18 pounds (8 kilograms)

LIFESPAN: 17 years

CHARACTER: curious, affectionate, intelligent

Designer
Breeds

Many cat breeds have begun as a mutation of a gene—part of the makeup of every living creature, including humans—and developed naturally. But there are also some breeds that have been "designed" by human hand.

THE BENGAL

The breathtakingly beautiful Bengal is the result of crossing a domestic cat with the wild Asian leopard cat. In fact, its name comes from the leopard cat's scientific name, *Prionailurus bengalensis*. The breed was started in California in the 1960s by Jean Mill. The modern Bengal can be traced back to the cats that she bred in the 1980s.

DARK ROSETTES

Mill wanted to produce a new breed that combined the gentle nature of a cuddly pet cat with the striking markings of the leopard, jaguar, and ocelot. The Bengal is the only domestic cat with contrasting dark rosettes on its golden coat. It also comes in a marbled pattern, which looks a little like a snow leopard.

FACT FILE

COLOR: brown tabby, seal mink tabby, black silver tabby, and seal silver lynx point, also marbled

EYE COLOR: green, yellow, gold, blue, aqua

SIZE (MALE ADULT): 15 pounds (7 kilograms)

LIFESPAN: 16 years

CHARACTER: alert, lively, affectionate

STRENGTH AND ELEGANCE

As well as having a glorious coat, which is soft as velvet to the touch, the Bengal is lean, lithe, and well-muscled. This breed is a wonderful mixture of strength and elegance. Its regal beauty is hard to resist, and its personality is enchanting. Despite its wild appearance, the Bengal is an affectionate, friendly cat that loves to interact with its humans.

CALM TEMPERAMENT

Modern breeders do their best to pair males and females that have the best of the breed—not only the beauty but also the calm temperament. As perhaps the highest profile "designer" breed, the Bengal is in great demand. One was reported to have sold for more than $50,000 in 1990. The Bengal is truly the Rolls-Royce of cats!

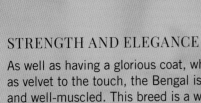

THE CHAUSIE

Cats were so valued in ancient Egypt that they have been found mummified in tombs. They were buried with their masters, to travel with them to the afterlife. Some of those long-dead remains were found to be a wild species known as the jungle cat. The goddess Bastet, who was worshipped by the ancient Egyptians, is said to be the model of a jungle cat.

ATHLETIC GRACE

The Chausie (pronounced "chow-see") is the result of deliberate cross-breeding between jungle cats and domestic cats. Its name comes from the jungle cat's scientific name, *Felis chaus*, and it has that animal's athletic grace and sleek, muscular body. It can move with speed and jump with ease—as high as 8 feet (2.4 meters)!

LOTS OF INTERACTION

Some people describe the Chausie as dog-like in its devotion to humans. It will play fetch with you and walk on a leash. But it doesn't do well left on its own; it needs lots of interaction. It is curious and wants to be involved in everything you do, and can even be taught tricks! A bored Chausie, left on its own, could get up to all sorts of mischief...

FACT FILE

COLOR: brown ticked tabby, black, black grizzled ticked tabby

EYE COLOR: gold, yellow, light green, hazel

SIZE (MALE ADULT): 20 pounds (9 kilograms)

LIFESPAN: 14 years

CHARACTER: curious, affectionate, lively

TUFTED EARS

There are only three recognized colors of Chausie—brown ticked tabby, black, and black grizzled ticked tabby. All three of these patterns are found in the wild jungle cat. Kittens are born with spots and stripes that fade as the cat matures, leaving a ticked coat with barring or stripes on the legs and tail. It sometimes has the tufted ears of a cougar.

THE RAGAMUFFIN

Are the Ragdoll and the RagaMuffin related? You bet they are! But the pretty RagaMuffin is accepted as a separate breed. The RagaMuffin has all the cuddly appeal of its cousin, and is described as a "heavily furred rabbit," with an adorable ruff around its neck and fluffy "knickerbockers" on its hind legs.

LOVING NATURE

The RagaMuffin can be traced back to the founder of the Ragdoll, Ann Baker. Cat breeders who worked with Baker decided to create their own breed, with the same sweet temper and loving nature, but more colors. They used a variety of different breeds as outcrosses, including domestic longhairs, Persians, and Himalayans, to widen the genetic pool of the new breed.

RAINBOW CATS

The result is a large, muscular cat with a stocky rectangular body, broad chest, and powerful shoulders supporting a short neck. The RagaMuffin has a broad head and an extravagantly fluffy tail. It comes in a variety of patterns and a rainbow of colors, including seal, chocolate, blue, lilac, black, red, silver, shaded, smoke, cameo, cream, and tortoiseshell.

PUPPY-LIKE FOLLOWER

Many cats, no matter how loving they may be, don't really like to be picked up. But the RagaMuffin loves to be hugged and cuddled! It is almost puppy-like in its desire to follow you around and be with you. It will snuggle into your arms like a baby, and it is always excited to see you.

FACT FILE

COLOR: all colors and patterns

EYE COLOR: blue, green, gold, amber, aqua

SIZE (MALE ADULT):
20 pounds (9 kilograms)

LIFESPAN: 16 years

CHARACTER: calm, patient, loving

THE HAVANA

Sometimes called the Havana brown, this cat is distinguished by the shape of its head, which is longer than it is wide. People have said that its mahogany-brown coat is the same rich color as a cigar called a Havana. The coat sets off the cat's glowing green eyes, and it has the lean, muscular body of a Siamese.

MYSTERIOUS ORIGINS

Mystery surrounds the Havana. Brown-colored cats were shown in England as far back as the 1800s, and a group of British breeders developed the Havana using a mix of dark-colored Siamese, Russian Blues, and black domestic shorthairs. The parents of the first registered Havana were a seal point Siamese and a black shorthair.

AMERICAN COUSINS

The new breed was originally called the chestnut foreign shorthair, but the name was changed to Havana in 1970. Breeders imported chestnut foreign shorthair cats to the United States, where they founded the Havana brown. There is a big difference between the English and American Havanas.

FACT FILE

COLOR: chocolate brown or lilac brown

EYE COLOR: green

SIZE (MALE ADULT):
10 pounds (4.5 kilograms)

LIFESPAN: 15 years

CHARACTER: affectionate, intelligent, people-oriented

SURPRISINGLY HEAVY

The English Havana is shaped more like a Siamese, while the American version has upright ears, a long muzzle, and an angular profile. It comes in both the original rich brown and a softer pinkish-gray color, called lilac. Both colors are set off by the Havana's mesmerizing green eyes. Picking up a Havana is surprising because it weighs more than it looks.

THE HIMALAYAN

Take a Siamese and add the luxurious fluff of the Persian, and you get a Himalayan. Clyde Keeler, a medical researcher, and a breeder named Virginia Cobb found the magic mixture that produced a longhaired cat with the distinctive colorpoint markings of the Siamese and the charm of the quiet and gentle Persian.

WINNING RECIPE

The first recognized Himalayan kitten was called Newton's Debutante. From those early experiments, more Himalayans—called Himmies for short— were bred, using the same process as Cobb and Keeler had developed. Once the colorpoint pattern—dark ears, legs, feet, tail, and face mask—was established, the cat was bred back to a Persian to get the desired long coat.

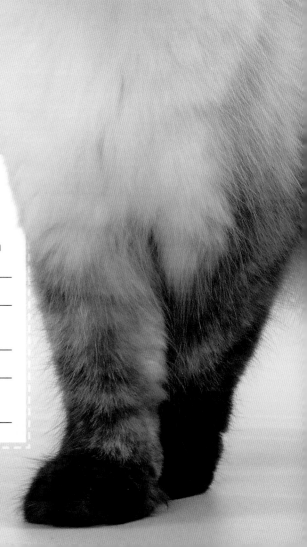

FACT FILE

COLOR: all colors, but there must be a contrast between body and point color

EYE COLOR: blue

SIZE (MALE ADULT): 12 pounds (5.5 kilograms)

LIFESPAN: 15 years

CHARACTER: sweet, loving, placid

HIMALAYAN HOPE

One breeder, Marguerita Goforth, is recognized as a "Himmie pioneer." She used a longhaired cat with seal point coloring called Princess Himalayan Hope to start a breeding program. Her efforts led to the Championship and American associations recognizing the Himalayan cat in 1957.

CUDDLY CAT

Himmies are a medium-sized stocky breed with a solid little body that is equally wide across the shoulders and the rump. The head is round and broad, set on a short, thick neck. A Himalayan's double-layered coat needs frequent grooming, but otherwise it is a low-maintenance cat. It loves to get plenty of cuddles, and it is more likely to climb into your lap than climb the curtains.

INDEX